IMAGES
of America

THE DUPONT
HIGHWAY

This is an artist's rendition of Thomas Coleman du Pont's "Grand Boulevard." T. Coleman had traveled to Europe and seen its wide avenues, built not only for transportation but for aesthetic value as well. He envisioned his north-south highway through Delaware with a 200-foot right-of-way, room enough for a two-way road for car traffic and another roadway for trucks, north and southbound trolley service, horse-riding trail, and a pedestrian walkway lined with trees. (Delaware State Archives.)

ON THE COVER: The Dupont Highway and Route 13 are pictured looking north at the junction with Route 40 in 1931. The photograph was taken from atop a railroad overpass. Hares Corner, located about one mile north of this intersection (by the New Castle County Airport) was a common destination for travelers coming south and west from the two major roads. Hares Corner was a former stage stop and cattle market named for a tavern operated by John Haire in the 1800s. In 1925, Routes 13, 113, and 40 were classified and designated as the only interstate highways in Delaware. (Delaware State Archives.)

IMAGES
of America

THE DUPONT HIGHWAY

William Francis and Michael C. Hahn

ARCADIA
PUBLISHING

Published by Arcadia Publishing
Charleston SC, Chicago IL, Portsmouth NH, San Francisco CA

Printed in the United States of America

Library of Congress Catalog Card Number: 2008941208

For all general information contact Arcadia Publishing at:
Telephone 843-853-2070
Fax 843-853-0044
E-mail sales@arcadiapublishing.com
For customer service and orders:
Toll-Free 1-888-313-2665

Visit us on the Internet at www.arcadiapublishing.com

*From William to Michele: thank you for your help and support always.
And to my coauthor, Michael C. Hahn, thank you for agreeing to be
part of my wild idea.*

CONTENTS

ACKNOWLEDGMENTS

The Delaware State Highway Department was created by the state's general assembly on April 2, 1917, in response to the 1916 Federal Aid Highway Act signed by Pres. Woodrow Wilson. The act granted funds for road-building but only to states with a professional highway department. By this time, the number of automobile registrations in the country had reached 2.3 million. The 1916 act marked the first time the federal government became directly involved in road-building efforts. Approximately $5 million was appropriated the first year. Funding reached $75 million by 1922.

The Delaware State Highway Department evolved into the Delaware Department of Transportation. Known as DELDOT for short, the agency is responsible for maintenance and operations for most of Delaware's public roads and bridges.

The authors wish to extend their sincere gratitude to the Hagley Museum and Library for use of its collection related to Thomas Coleman du Pont and his highway and to the Delaware State Archives for use of its DELDOT collection and other materials for the purpose of this book. We greatly appreciate the time and effort the staffs of both libraries put in on our behalf, especially Lori Hatch at the state archives. We also wish to thank the Delaware Department of Agriculture, the Delaware Department of Transportation, the Delaware State Police Museum, and Michele Mahoney for the assistance she provided.

All images in this book—except where noted—are courtesy of the Delaware State Archives, Dover, Delaware.

INTRODUCTION

It is difficult to imagine in this era of superhighways and multicar ownership that it was not long ago when people traveled and shipped goods by horse, rail, or boat. The few roads that existed were often dirt and gravel, or thick mud in bad weather, poorly maintained, and rutted by wheels from early motorized vehicles.

Up until 1920, the average working man's salary was less than $1,500 a year. Automobiles were handmade, piece by piece and one vehicle at a time. They could cost $3,000 to $10,000. Henry Ford institutionalized the assembly line method of automobile manufacturing, and his Model T Ford sold for less than $300. Vehicular ownership rose. Motorists and bicyclists organized and petitioned legislatures for better roads and more surface transportation routes, what historians have called the "Good Roads Movement." The U.S. Congress responded with the creation of the Bureau of Public Roads and then the Federal Highway Administration. The agencies began as part of the U.S. Department of Agriculture but eventually fell under the U.S. Department of Transportation.

Thomas Coleman du Pont, great-grandson of the DuPont Company's founder, Eleuthère Irénée du Pont, was an early proponent of the automobile. He was a native of Kentucky and graduated from the Massachusetts Institute of Technology in 1885 as a civil engineer. He returned to Kentucky and soon rose to superintendent of the Central Coal and Iron Company. He spent time in Johnstown, Pennsylvania, with a company that made street railway cars. By the age of 37, T. Coleman du Pont had made a fortune in coal, steel, insurance, and commercial real estate. In 1902, the centennial year of the DuPont Company's founding as a gunpowder manufacturer along the Brandywine River in Wilmington, the family business was almost sold to a competitor. T. Coleman, along with cousins Pierre S. du Pont and Alfred I. du Pont, took control of the company. But T. Coleman du Pont hadn't forgotten his love of the automobile, nor his realization that Delaware roads, particularly downstate, were primitive at best. T. Coleman du Pont offered to build a "Grand Boulevard" the length of Delaware at no cost to the public and then donate the road to the state. He felt a hard-surface road was necessary to spur economic growth and prosperity and would especially benefit the farmers of Kent and Sussex Counties, who had only the monopoly of the railroads available to ship their produce. To fulfill his aspirations, T. Coleman achieved legislative approval on March 31, 1911, to create a road construction company with the initial capital stock of $200,000. He was quoted in 1912 as saying, "Nothing can do more good than money spent in building or improving roads in the United States." Starting in Sussex County in 1911, T. Coleman personally supervised the first 30 miles of a two-lane concrete road that would bear his name.

Despite T. Coleman du Pont's best intentions, there was opposition, naturally, from railroad companies that saw the road as infringing on their business and political factions who believed T. Coleman was building the road for personal gain. There was even resistance from some farmers who felt the road was an "invasion" of their land. To quell opposition, T. Coleman offered property owners up to five times the assessed value of their property for a right-of-way, and in

1917, he agreed to turn the project over to the newly created Delaware Highway Department. Yet T. Coleman continued to fund the project up to $44,000 per mile. He eventually paid almost $4 million of his own money.

T. Coleman du Pont truly believed those with means should contribute to the betterment of society: "I realized that the first essential for the development of our little State is a well laid out system of highways traversing all the sections of the State. It was obvious from the beginning that the backbone of such a system must be a main north and south highway."

While other philanthropists started schools, libraries, parks, and hospitals, T. Coleman du Pont stated, "I will build a monument a hundred miles high and lay it on the ground." He was close. The two-lane concrete highway that bore Coleman du Pont's name measured 96.7 miles. The highway was on Delaware's map as Route 13 between Dover and Wilmington and as Route 113 between Dover and Selbyville at the state's southern border with Maryland. The Coleman DuPont Road was officially dedicated and given to the citizens of Delaware by Coleman du Pont during a ceremony held in Dover on July 2, 1924.

As a member of the original commission appointed by Gov. John Townsend, Coleman du Pont was also the first to realize that traffic on Delaware's highways was destined to approach in speed and volume that of the railroads. He had the courage and patience, despite opposition, to plan and construct the DuPont Highway with provisions for the future. With a right-of-way planned in many sections of 200 feet and bypassing all towns, and with curves and grades adequate for high-speed traffic, the highway after its first 20 years compared favorably with most modern superhighways of the early 20th century. DELDOT and the State of Delaware are left with his legacy of design and construction standards in solving and improving transportation issues of the state.

In 1927, the chief engineer for the Delaware State Highway Department, C. Douglass Buck, recommended reducing traffic congestion by expanding the Coleman DuPont Road into a dual highway between Dover and Wilmington, two lanes northbound and two lanes southbound with a grassy median in between, a common sight today but innovative at the time. When completed in 1934, the span between Dover and Wilmington became the country's first divided highway and a model for all highway construction since. It was also innovative in that it was the first thoroughfare laid near towns, not through them, in an effort to minimize downtown traffic.

By 1940, trucking had taken over as a main source for shipping Delaware's agricultural products, and the DuPont Highway was the principle route taken. In that year, over a million crates of poultry carrying over 19 million fowl, over 2 million bushels of potatoes, over 200,000 bushels of peaches, and almost a million crates of strawberries were hauled on the DuPont Highway. In one day, over 35,000 vehicles traveled the highway and carried more than 100,000 people. It was estimated that almost one-eighth of employed Delawareans had a dependence or business relationship with the DuPont Highway on a daily basis.

However, the DuPont Highway became a victim of its own success. Less than a decade after its dedication, the corridor had to be expanded to accommodate safety and the increase in automobile traffic. Ultimately, the road corridor led to business and housing development that absorbed all the land around it and created busy intersections. Senior Delawareans remember the highway as the main route to Delaware's beaches and how long a trip to sun and sand could take with the highway's congestion, varying speed limits, and numerous traffic signals. A new turnpike with limited access was needed.

State Road Route 1 was constructed between 1991 and 2004 and has surpassed the DuPont Highway in traffic volume and, in a few locations, caused segments of the DuPont Highway to be rerouted or abandoned. What is left of the DuPont Highway often parallels or crosses beneath Route 1 bridges and now resembles a local road, used by those who wish to travel at a slower pace, be nostalgic, or by commuters and beachgoers wishing to avoid the Route 1 tolls.

One

COLEMAN DUPONT ROAD

Thomas Coleman du Pont (1863–1930), a descendant of the DuPont Company founder, served as company president from 1902 to 1915. He also served as a fill-in U.S. senator from 1921 to 1922 upon the resignation of Joseph Wolcott. He later served as an elected senator from 1925 until ill health compelled him to resign in 1928. He was the founder of Wilmington Trust Bank. The DuPont Highway remains the greatest personal gift in the history of the Delaware Highway Department. (Hagley Museum and Library.)

No roadside assistance was available for this stranded motorist on a "main highway" to Georgetown in Sussex County in 1912. Drivers ventured out at their own risk following even a light rain because roads were not graded and were poorly maintained. Most road-building and maintenance fell under the jurisdiction of local towns or Levy Court. In 1903, the Delaware General Assembly passed the State Aid Road Law, which for the first time appropriated matching funds for road construction. (Hagley Museum and Library.)

Many of the state's early roads developed from trails laid out by the native Lenni Lenape Indians. The natives had established a network of trails for trading, hunting, and moving from village to village. Europeans who colonized Delaware in the 1600s, primarily Swedish, Finnish, Dutch, and English, utilized many of these trails and expanded them. Other early roads had to be surveyed and mapped out where ground and site conditions varied. (Hagley Museum and Library.)

This is an 1880 artist's rendition of the DuPont Company gunpowder mills along the Brandywine River in Wilmington, Delaware. The DuPont Corporation was founded in 1802 by Eleuthère Irénée du Pont. Eleuthère and his family had left France two years earlier to escape the French Revolution. As president of the company, T. Coleman du Pont bought out the competition and achieved a monopoly on the production and distribution of military-grade smokeless gunpowder and commercial high explosives. (Hagley Museum and Library.)

A realistic view of the Eleutherian Mills Powder Yard along the Brandywine River in the 1880s includes a residence (upper left), saltpeter refinery (center), and charcoal house (upper right). Gunpowder production was a dangerous business. In 1818, forty workers were killed by an explosion that injured mill workers' children who attended an on-site school. A year earlier, the elderly Pierre Samuel du Pont died after battling a fire at the mill. Alexis du Pont was killed fighting a fire in 1857. (Hagley Museum and Library.)

Coleman du Pont's residence was in the 800 block of Broom Street in Wilmington. Coleman du Pont died there from cancer of the larynx on November 11, 1930. The property was sold in 1939 for $35,000 and is now the site of the Holy Trinity Greek Orthodox Church. Coleman du Pont owned several properties during his lifetime; one was the historic Buena Vista alongside his highway near the Routes 13 and 40 interchange. Coleman purchased Buena Vista in 1914 for $35,000 and remained its owner until his death. (Hagley Museum and Library.)

Coleman du Pont saw many marginal farms and their produce stands during his trips to and from a hunting lodge he owned at Horn Point on Maryland's Eastern Shore. It convinced him that the lives and incomes of Delaware farmers would be greatly enhanced if they could move their perishables faster and safer to urban markets such as Wilmington, Philadelphia, New York, and Washington, D.C. Sussex County businessman John G. Townsend (elected governor in 1916) assisted with right-of-way acquisitions through his partnership with Peninsula Real Estate Company, Inc.

The Coleman DuPont Road incorporated some existing roads, especially when it later expanded as U.S. Route 13 north of Wilmington up to the Pennsylvania state line. In particular, this arched stone bridge over Naaman's Creek was built in 1919 and was part of the Philadelphia and Wilmington Turnpike.

This photograph is believed to be looking north in the vicinity of south Wilmington. As chairman of the Board of National Councilors of the National Highway Association, Coleman du Pont was not the only advocate for good roads. The Good Roads Movement was a collection of people, primarily bicyclists and leading politicians, such as Teddy Roosevelt, who believed America would improve economically and come closer together as a nation if linked by good roads. The influence of the automobile, and the auto clubs that followed, pushed the notion of "good roads everywhere" into the political arena. Coleman du Pont used his organizations as leverage to achieve a modern road system that would operate under a federal interstate highway system (similar to the Federal Highway Administration today). The National Highway Association believed a local system, even supported by federal monies, would be too responsive to local pressure and would not be a long-term benefit to the nation. Coleman du Pont decided in 1908 to show the nation how to build a modern road.

With hard-surface road-building in its infancy, time and labor saving devices had not yet become commonplace. Clearing this right-of-way above Drawyer's Creek north of Odessa around 1920 required an army of men and animals. Mule teams and the wagons attached were used like the modern dump truck to haul away dirt removed from the hillside during grading.

The Coleman DuPont Road was initially started through Coleman's private company. By the time of this construction north of Odessa, the Delaware State Highway Department had assumed control of the project and pledged to complete it under the leadership of C. Douglass Buck (1890–1965). Buck assisted as an engineer for Colemen du Pont and served afterwards as chief engineer for the highway department from 1921 until 1928. Buck later became Coleman du Pont's son-in-law and Delaware's governor from 1929 to 1937. Coleman du Pont also had his son Francis V. assist as an engineer. Francis V. du Pont served as chairman for the state highway department and later became chief of the Bureau of Public Roads under Pres. Dwight D. Eisenhower. Under Eisenhower, Francis V. became responsible for supervising the construction of the modern interstate system.

Of course, prior to any road construction, a survey crew had to be employed to chart the route. Coleman du Pont championed the old adage that the shortest distance between two points is a straight line. The Coleman DuPont Road was noteworthy for its long stretches of straight road. Coleman du Pont had two rules for his workers: "1. If you want anything necessary to the building of the road, get it. 2. Hurry, not a fraction of a minute wasted." This survey crew obviously is not cooperating with rule No. 2.

Anything To Block Progress

This editorial cartoon appeared in the Wilmington *Sunday Star* on March 24, 1912. The *Sunday Star* favored the road. The Wilmington *Evening Journal* opposed it. Although Coleman du Pont started his road-building company in 1911 and ground had been broken near Selbyville, it would be 13 more years before his road was officially dedicated. Construction was often delayed by legal and political wrangling. A frustrated Coleman du Pont said, "I don't know whether the people of Delaware want the road or not. If they don't want it, I don't want to spend money necessary to give it to them."

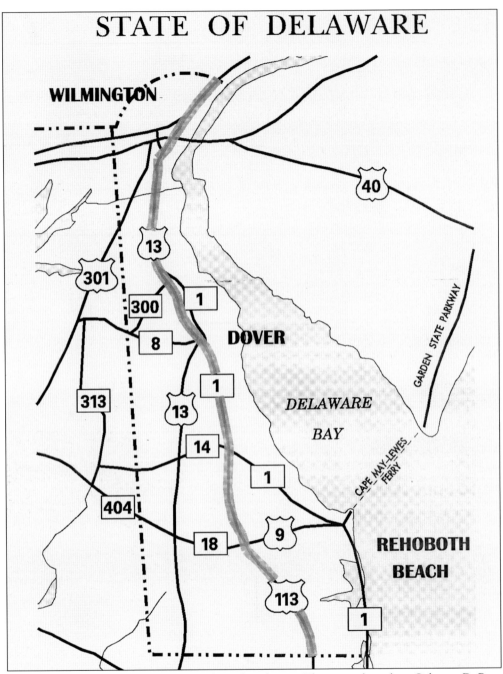

STATE OF DELAWARE

WILMINGTON

40

13

301

300

1

8

DOVER

1

13

313

14

1

404

18

9

113

1

DELAWARE BAY

GARDEN STATE PARKWAY

CAPE MAY–LEWES FERRY

REHOBOTH BEACH

Here is the route of the DuPont Highway through Delaware. The original two-lane Coleman DuPont Road did not extend north of Wilmington and received the U.S. route number designations 13 and 113 in 1925, when the road was incorporated into the national highway network in response to the Federal Highway Act of 1921. The act called for the construction of state highways to link and unify as an interstate system. (DELDOT Mapping.)

The Coleman DuPont Road was concrete and fitted to a mold much like the modern sidewalk. Men at work are stretched out on benches using ordinary hand trowels to smooth the surface. The 14-foot road had no curbs or striping, limited roadside drainage, and dirt shoulders. When two vehicles approaching at opposite directions met, one or both vehicles would have to ride partially on the unpaved shoulder to pass by. (Hagley Museum and Library.)

Since "the shortest distance between two points is a straight line," trees were cleared when necessary. However, the Coleman DuPont Road and its successor, the DuPont Highway, eventually planted more trees than were removed in response to Coleman du Pont and the state highway department's desire to make the highway aesthetically pleasing. (Hagley Museum and Library.)

COLEMAN DU PONT ROAD

—INCORPORATED—

SELBYVILLE TO GEORGETOWN

APPROVED

_____ _____ ___ _Governor_
_____ _____ ___ _Lieut. Governor_
_____ _____ ___ _Secretary of State_

Known as Contract RM 1, the Coleman DuPont Road, Inc., was the first of a series of eight original roadway surveys and construction segments instituted or planned by Coleman du Pont. Survey and design plans were dated in 1911, but the first construction started from Selbyville to Georgetown in 1912. Contract RM 2 under the Coleman DuPont Road, Inc., from Georgetown to Milford (actually 6 miles prior to Milford) was the second and last segment solely engineered, administered, and financed by the Coleman DuPont Road, Inc. The two contract segments began at the same time. The combined efforts consisted of approximately 29 miles. Thereafter, and by 1917, other segments of the Coleman DuPont Road, Inc., were just surveys in preparation of the new or improved highway. The newly formed state highway department would later design, construct, administer, and finance any extras to complete the DuPont Highway from south Milford to Wilmington. By 1918, Coleman du Pont and the State of Delaware agreed to dissolve the company, but du Pont continued to finance the remaining segments of the highway north to Wilmington at a "cost not to exceed $44,000 per mile." This effort did not include bridge and approach work over the Chesapeake and Delaware Canal because of charters rewritten with the canal company. (DELDOT Contract Archives.)

Initially serving as chief engineer of his corporation's project, Coleman du Pont had a 1911 Stoddard-Dayton "Camping Car" built to his specifications so he could live along corridor and construction sites and personally supervise the work on his highway. The 45-horsepower car had a 115-inch wheelbase. The waterproof silk tent protected an interior that contained room enough for a 6-foot bed, work space, and storage lockers. (Hagley Museum and Library.)

Coleman du Pont's engineers and supervisors pose on the porch of a house in Georgetown, Sussex County. Coleman du Pont brought in European highway engineers—Ernest Storms from Belgium and Thomas Aitken from Scotland—as consultants. Frank Williams, chief engineer for the Highway Department of New York, was appointed chief engineer for the project. The Good Roads Movement and his involvement with the National Highway Association enhanced Coleman's ideas on where to locate the highway, what material to use to build his road, and who to hire as engineers and consulting personnel. (Hagley Museum and Library.)

While Coleman du Pont had his camping car and his staff had a house for headquarters, some of the workers on remote sites lived in temporary housing or work camps, as seen here. Several construction men quartering in one shelter was common. (Hagley Museum and Library.)

Here is the same temporary housing for the workers on the Coleman DuPont Road, now a wintry scene with snow covering the ground and an American flag proudly displayed on the roof. The men kept warm with the aid of wood stoves placed inside the building. (Hagley Museum and Library.)

There were also less solid structures built in the work camps, as this snow-covered tent will attest. Snow and cold temperatures stopped construction. There were no road plows to clear the way. The workers had to entertain themselves during such long periods of inactivity. Keeping warm, card playing, drinking, and the occasional fight were part of the job. (Hagley Museum and Library.)

In this image of a supply depot at Millsboro in Sussex County are a water tower in the background and a stone and gravel hopper in the foreground. Because there were no construction vehicles such as dump trucks, bulldozers, or backhoes, road-building supplies were brought to the construction sites either by horse, mule, oxen, or by railcar on temporary rail lines. In this photograph, gravel is dumped into the funnel-like hopper, allowing the gravel to be evenly distributed in the railcars. (Hagley Museum and Library.)

A steam-powered tractor was used to haul freight and supplies to road-building sites. Steam-powered tractors were designed for agricultural use in the late 1800s and early 1900s. The steam-engine tractor was gradually phased out by the mid-1920s as the internal-combustion engine tractors emerged following World War I. (Hagley Museum and Library.)

This c. 1920 truck had its flatbed modified with steel rails in order to haul away empty railcars and return them to the hopper. The empty cars were pushed away from the building site, then up a ramp and onto elevated rails visible behind the truck. The truck backed up against the end of the elevated rail (in the background) to receive the cars.

Here is a rear view of a truck bed backed up against the elevated railway and being loaded with the empty railcars. Once the steel tracks were lined up, it was a matter of manpower to complete the transfer from track to truck. Men who worked in mining were right at home with these railcars, as they were similar to those used to haul away minerals taken from beneath the earth's surface.

A steam-powered train makes its delivery to the work site at the Ellendale forest area in Sussex County in 1918, located halfway between Milford and Georgetown. Ellendale's economy as a leading railroad and shipping center was adversely affected by the opening of the Coleman DuPont Road. (Hagley Museum and Library.)

Known as "narrow gauge" because the track gauge is less than the standard gauge commonly used by freight and passenger train service, narrow-gauge rails are commonly used in mountainous terrain for quarrying and mining. Narrow-gauge rails are lighter, cheaper, and easier to assemble and dismantle. The use of narrow-gauge rails in road construction disappeared because of the capabilities of modern trucks. (Hagley Museum and Library.)

The men are working with a Koehring steam-driven concrete mixer. The Koehring Machine Company of Milwaukee, Wisconsin, was founded in 1907. Koehring marketed six models of concrete mixers c. 1910 with capacities from 10 to 30 cubic feet based on dry batched material. The 5- to 12-horsepower steam engines had operating weights from 7,300 to 15,000 pounds. (Hagley Museum and Library.)

When steam-driven trains or tractors were not available to haul supplies to the work site, horses, mules, and oxen were used. Here bags and bags of foundation stone are delivered and dumped. (Hagley Museum and Library.)

Men are at work on the Coleman DuPont Road. The "dump" car can be tilted in order to transfer the stone to the building site. Laid over a bed of compacted soil and crushed gravel, concrete is the most durable road-surfacing material. (Hagley Museum and Library.)

In the Ellendale vicinity in 1918, a popular Koehring mixer was model No. 15 with a 15-cubic-foot dry-batch capacity. It was equipped with a 30-inch-diameter vertical boiler 6 feet 6 inches high and a vertical steam engine with 5½-inch bore and 7-inch stroke, developing 7 horsepower at 253 revolutions per minute. The side loader bucket could be raised in 8 seconds, and the mixer emptied the wet concrete in 18 seconds. The company claimed Model No. 15 could produce 180 cubic yards of concrete in a 10-hour day. (Hagley Museum and Library.)

The Koehring mixer had a convenient design for the times. Several mixing actions occurred within the drum because it had been fitted with two sets of baffle blades. Also the discharge chute reached deep inside the drum and rotated 90 degrees on a horizontal axis, so in one position, it discharged the drum contents or, in the opposite position, aided the mixing process by directing the rotating material to the opposite side of the drum. (Hagley Museum and Library.)

This chute position, combined with the two sets of baffle blades, caused the material inside the Koehring mixer to move continually in the drum from front to back, as well as being rotated and showered to the bottom of the drum at each rotation. (Hagley Museum and Library.)

Workmen had to hand-shovel cement and aggregate dry mix into wheelbarrows that also served as measuring devices needed to load the skip hoist for the Koehring concrete mixer. Two bags of dry mix produced approximately 11 cubic feet. (Hagley Museum and Library.)

The wet concrete mix leaves the Koehring mixer and is sent down the chute, where it becomes filler between the established mold. Concrete is a material composed of cement, usually Portland cement, as well as a coarse aggregate, such as gravel or limestone and sand. Concrete is the world's most commonly used man-made material. (Hagley Museum and Library.)

The Coleman DuPont Road was an early user of wire reinforcement in its concrete. The steel mesh was delivered in rolls and cut into sheets and weighed about .65 pounds per square foot. From 1915 to 1917, the road south of Georgetown was reinforced with 400-foot-long slabs of welded wire. This later proved to be too long and inadequate for the weight of traffic. (Hagley Museum and Library.)

When it came to wire mesh reinforcement, there was disagreement over whether or not triangular woven mesh, as seen in this photograph, or rectangular woven mesh worked best. Both styles were deemed interchangeable and provided a good mechanical bond for the concrete. (Hagley Museum and Library.)

The men in the foreground are "spading" the wet concrete, poking the shovel in and out of the wet mix, necessary to consolidate the cement. Consolidation eliminates rock pockets and air bubbles and brings enough fine material to the surface and against the perimeter mold to produce the desired finish. (Hagley Museum and Library.)

A lot of manual labor had to be employed to construct the Coleman DuPont Road. Work began just south of Georgetown in September 1911. The area was selected only because it was the first section of land to be legally available for building. Securing rights-of-way was a constant problem prior to the state highway department taking over the project. While many rights-of-way were donated (since it was a benefit), others refuted. Coleman du Pont and his corporation paid up to five times the real assessed value to secure linear rights-of-way. Sections between Selbyville and the Appenzeller Farm six miles south of Milford (Contracts RM 1 and RM 2) were completed by 1917. (Hagley Museum and Library.)

An excellent view shows the entire road-building process during the concrete phase. Crates of dry mix were hoisted and loaded into the mixer. The mixer deposits the wet concrete on the road while empty crates are pushed forward down the temporary rails. Men smooth the wet concrete and place strategic expansion separators at equal distances.

The men in the foreground manually vibrate the leveler over the wet cement to help spread the wet mix and fit it to the form, a process called "screeding." (Hagley Museum and Library.)

A step up from the two-man leveler, this vibrating strike machine screeded and consolidated the concrete. New road-building devices, meant to save time and cost and reduce physical labor, developed as a result of what was learned by building not only the Coleman DuPont Road but other highway projects throughout the United States.

In the 1920s, concrete was cured by this example of "ponding." Water-bound concrete left to dry on its own will not bond sufficiently. A dam of dirt and sand was built and water added and left to set for a day or two. This method could produce stains on the concrete if impure water was used. However, this made the road essentially waterproof and economical to maintain.

Before any road can be laid, the ground surface must be tested for its strength and viability. The gentlemen pictured here are taking bore samples, testing the soil by drilling a hole in the surface and observing how quickly a volume of water dissipates into the subsoil. The Coleman DuPont Road filled in a number of existing wetlands. (Hagley Museum and Library.)

The Ellendale Swamp, as it was known, was the greatest stretch of wetlands and drainage pockets needing to be rechanneled, drained, and filled in order to solidify the ground surface for the Coleman DuPont Road. The men are excavating a channel or rechanneling a small tributary for placement of a small culvert or lateral pipes across the future road. Throughout the Ellendale area, several small drainage structures and larger tax ditches were necessary to help facilitate a safe passage through this relatively remote section of the highway. Prior to the Coleman DuPont Road, Ellendale was one of the worst spots for a traveler. It was common for horses, men, and automobiles to be rescued from the inundation of the unpredictable soils and traveling surfaces. (Hagley Museum and Library.)

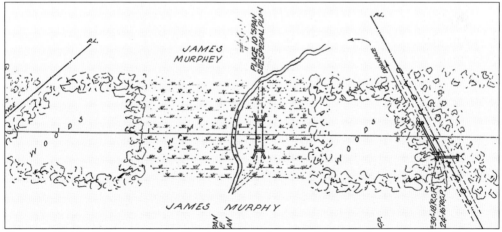

Contract RM 2, Coleman DuPont Road, Inc., was the second (original) segment of the Coleman DuPont Road between Georgetown and Milford, completed in 1917. Continued north in 1918 by the state highway department, State Contract 8 detailed the road's centerline within the more difficult sections of the Ellendale Swamp that had to be cleared, graded, and constructed with adequate drainage structures. (DELDOT Archive Plans.)

The Coleman DuPont Road ended in south Wilmington by Rodgers Corner. The county and city had existing roads that connected their ports and industries, mostly north to Pennsylvania, such as the Newport Gap Turnpike, Kennett Pike, and Concord Pike, and a road south to New Castle and Christiana. Pictured here is excavation for what would become part of the DuPont Highway, Route 13, in the Penny Hill section of Wilmington.

In 1929, the installation of underground telephone conduits occurred between Wilmington and Dover along the Coleman DuPont Road. Gas lines were also installed between Dover, Cheswold, Smyrna, and Clayton. The Coleman DuPont Road assisted not only transportation needs, but brought advancement, modern improvements, and convenience to those living on farms and in rural communities.

A man stands guard on a stretch of "ponding" road between St. Georges and Tybout's Corner in New Castle County in 1922. Notice how straight the road is and the many levels of wires supported by the utility poles lining the roadside. Utility poles have been around since the advent of the telegraph in the mid-1800s.

Prior to any "ponding," however, the road between St. Georges and Tybout's Corner had to be leveled and the mold put in place and ready for poured concrete. The road was the last segment of the original Coleman DuPont Road, Inc., that simply illustrated a survey base line under Contract RM 8 from St. Georges to Wilmington. Plan details were later designed and administered under the state highway department under Contracts 33 and 33A in 1922.

Construction of the Coleman DuPont Road occurs between Magnolia and Rising Sun in Kent County in 1922 under State Contract 16. This section of the Coleman DuPont Road, and most of the subsequent DuPont Highway between Dover and Milford, has been incorporated or superseded by sections of State Route 1. The contract consisted of a 14-foot road (similar to others) from Magnolia to Cooper's Corner for a distance of 4.92 miles.

In Sussex County in 1919, this is an early example of a steam-driven steamroller. The steamroller was similar to the tractor, except for its large cylinder drum in front, which was used to level the surface through a combination of the size and weight of the vehicle.

When it came to railroad tracks, crossed in a number of locations, engineers on the Coleman DuPont Road had to determine if it was better to put the highway at grade level with the railway or dig out and run the road beneath a bridge. In this case, the highway went under the bridge. This photograph, near State Road during the early 1920s, shows the road under State Contract 14 just south of the U.S. 13 and U.S. 40 intersection. Historically, this juncture also delineates where the Coleman DuPont Road became the first divided highway in the country with a grassy median in 1929.

By 1930, through traffic in Dover necessitated the creation of the first bypass route directly associated with the Coleman DuPont Road. In 1931, Contracts 168 and 168A established a 4.1-mile, 9-foot concrete road corridor from Little Heaven to Bay Road. Plans also prepared for a two-lane bascule span at Barkers Landing over the St. Jones River. After years of planning and design and delays in securing approval of the plans by the U.S. Army Corps of Engineers, work began on this structure in 1933. The bridge's contract was awarded to Snyder Engineering Company of Middlesex, New Jersey, at a cost of $72,242. The bridge consisted of an overhead counterweight similar to the Laurel and Milford bridges constructed in previous years. Originally, the 9-foot road supporting the bridge and bypass was considered adequate as a feeder road to the main system, and it had been built and designed so it could be immediately widened when traffic increased. (DELDOT Archive Plans.)

In preparation for a new bypass road to be built south of Dover to Little Heaven, it was necessary to cross 3,150 feet of marshland at Barker's Landing. The original borings showed depths of mud ranging from 3 to 54 feet. Nine hundred feet of wetlands was over 40 feet in depth. Work to stabilize the subsurface began in December 1931, and over 250,333 cubic yards of fill had to be placed. Previous to the fill placement, a heavy mat of marsh peat and wetland soil had to be broken up by use of dynamite. This was accomplished by blasting a trench along the centerline of the anticipated roadway. Fill placement work was completed in August 1932. In the spring of 1933, workers attempted to force the fill down with the use of more explosives. Mud pockets were plated, and gelatin dynamite was used. Additional fill material had to be placed.

Two

THE GIFT

Governor William D. Denney
and the
Committee in Charge
request your presence
at the formal opening of the
Coleman du Pont Road
Wednesday, the second of July
at two o'clock (Standard Time)
Dover, Delaware
1924

This card was presented to Coleman du Pont from Delaware governor William Denny and the Committee in Charge, requesting Coleman du Pont's presence in Dover on July 2, 1924, to take part in the formal dedication of the Coleman DuPont Road. (Hagley Museum and Library.)

A horse-drawn Conestoga wagon to represent an early form of transportation took part in the dedication parade in Dover. However, before making the 46-mile journey to the state capital, it waited outside the Hotel DuPont at Rodney Square in Wilmington. The wagon banner reads, "Going to Coleman du Pont Road Celebration." The wagon was on loan from Amos Gingrich of Lancaster, Pennsylvania. The elaborate Hotel DuPont opened January 15, 1913. (Hagley Museum and Library.)

It was a festive and patriotic day in Dover. Buildings, and the dignitaries' cars, were adorned in red, white, and blue bunting and American flags. An estimated 10,000 people viewed the dedication ceremony on "the Green" and watched the parade up State and Loockerman Streets. The ceremony was publicly advertised and was considered a formal affair with groups and organizations represented from different parts of the state. (Hagley Museum and Library.)

Members of the Walter Fox Post of the American Legion dressed in Revolutionary-era uniforms and marched in the parade along South State Street. Delaware prides itself as one of the original 13 colonies and the first state to approve the U.S. Constitution on December 7, 1787. Per capita, Delaware sent more soldiers to General Washington's army than any other colony. The fighting spirit and tenacity of the Delaware soldiers was compared to the fighting prowess of the Delaware gamecocks that traveled with the troop under Capt. John Caldwell. His regiment soon earned the nickname "The Fightin' Blue Hens." (Hagley Museum and Library.)

A float from the Wilmington Automobile Trade Association represented the Dutch settlement named Zwaanendael (Swan Valley), to which the town of Lewes traces its origin. Founded in 1631 as a whaling colony and trading post, Zwaanendael had 32 inhabitants, later killed by natives. Nevertheless, Lewes is credited as the first town in the First State. The float is parading down Loockerman Street in Dover, where one of Delaware's first established banks (Farmers Bank of Delaware) can be seen in the background. (Hagley Museum and Library.)

The Conestoga wagon arrived and took part in the parade in Dover. The capital of Delaware was decked out in red, white, and blue and displayed American and state of Delaware flags. A number of floats had been created by different towns and organizations to show their civic pride and their appreciation to Coleman du Pont.

The theme of the parade was modes of transportation throughout history—from horses to horse-drawn wagons and carriages to a variety of early motorized vehicles. However, participants couldn't help but advertise. The previous photograph had advertised an absolute auction of lots located in Rehoboth Heights. In this picture, the vehicle behind the tractor is announcing Ford as "No. 1."

The relatively new and growing trucking industry was represented by a vehicle from the Peninsula Auto Express Company, or PAX for short. Because of the Coleman DuPont Road, trucking supplanted trains and ships as the number one mode for moving goods and services throughout Delaware.

The town of Milton contributed an ox-drawn cart to the parade as a demonstration for the pioneering spirit of early Delaware. The person seated in the wagon is actually a man in a dress pretending to smoke a corncob pipe. Their banner represents them as the most common form of transportation in Milton in 1894.

An ambulance and nurses from Beebe Hospital in Lewes took part in the ceremony and were available just in case someone needed medical attention. They were also present to advertise the Beebe School of Nursing, which opened in 1921 and continues today. The photograph was taken near the Kent County Courthouse on the Green. (Hagley Museum and Library.)

The Coleman DuPont Road gave birth to the Delaware State Police, pictured in front of the Supreme Court Building. The first traffic law enforcement officers had the title Highway Traffic Police. In 1919, Highway Traffic Police had only one officer, and his sole function was to patrol the Philadelphia Pike near Wilmington. The Delaware General Assembly created the Delaware State Police on April 23, 1923. During 1924–1925, the state police had five facilities: Penny Hill, Station No. 1; State Road, Station No. 2; Dover, Station No. 3; Georgetown, Station No. 4; and Bridgeville, Station No. 5.

A group of Nanticoke Indians from Oak Orchard in Sussex County took part in the parade. They were originally called Kuskarawaoks, meaning "tidewater people" in the Algonquian language. The first European reported to have seen the tribe was Capt. John Smith in 1608 during his travels throughout the Chesapeake Bay and its environs. After some tense initial moments, the natives befriended Captain Smith and his men, and some served as guides as Smith continued his exploration of the Chesapeake region. Captain Smith called the Nanticokes "the best merchants of all." (Both Hagley Museum and Library.)

Whereas; Coleman du Pont has created and presented to the State of Delaware a State Highway, and Whereas; on Wednesday July second 1924 the State of Delaware will, in Dover, publicly thank Coleman du Pont for his princely gift;
Therefore be it resolved that the Town Council of Dover in Special Session met this twenty-third day of June A.D. 1924 extends the freedom of the Town of Dover to Coleman du Pont in token of its gratitude for and appreciation of his great gift; and
Be it further resolved that this resolution be spread upon the minutes of Council and a copy thereof be presented to Mr. du Pont.

A resolution from the Dover Town Council expressing their gratitude and appreciation for Coleman du Pont's gift to the state was passed during a special session on June 23, 1924, and presented to Coleman du Pont. He responded with a letter the day after the dedication. It was read by Mayor J. C. Hopkins to the Dover City Council on July 7: "I just want to go on record to thank you very much for giving me the freedom of the city and keys to your town, which, of course, must include the key to the jail, had I gotten into trouble. I appreciate so much and congratulate you as mayor of Dover, on the charming hospitality displayed by your city." (Hagley Museum and Library.)

The dedication ceremony took place at the Green, on the grounds of the Old State House. Then-senator Coleman du Pont is pictured in the middle of the podium. Shaking hands is Benjamin Franklin Courtright (left), who is impersonating Caesar Rodney, a Revolutionary-era figure and signer of the Declaration of Independence. The dedication ceremony took place on the 148th anniversary of Caesar Rodney's historic ride from Dover to Philadelphia to cast his vote in favor of the Declaration of Independence. Also shaking hands is James Davis, secretary of labor in Calvin Coolidge's administration. (Hagley Museum and Library.)

On the podium presenting a silver plaque from the Citizens of Delaware to Sen. Coleman du Pont are Secretary of Labor James Davis (left), governor of Delaware William Denney, and on the right, Judge George Grey of Wilmington. The plaque is sterling silver and had been made by Tiffany and Company in New York. It depicts a map of Delaware with a gold line representing the north-south route of the Coleman DuPont Road. (Hagley Museum and Library.)

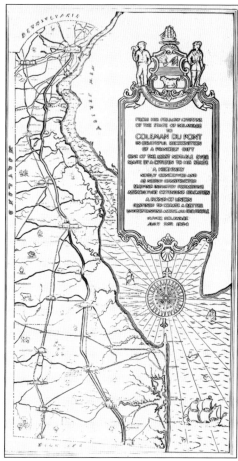

The silver plaque presented to Senator Coleman du Pont during the ceremony shows the state of Delaware, the Delaware River, the location of major towns and railroads, and of course the route of the Coleman DuPont Road virtually down the middle of the state. The plaque is currently displayed at the State Archives Building in Dover. (Hagley Museum and Library.)

On the steps to the Delaware State House, July 2, 1924, are, from left to right, (first row) Alice du Pont Buck, Katherine du Pont, Mrs. Coleman (Alice) du Pont, and Renee du Pont Donaldson; (second row) C. Douglass Buck, Halladay Meede, Francis V. du Pont, and Sen. Coleman du Pont. Coleman du Pont married Alice du Pont, a second cousin, on January 17, 1889, and had five children. (Hagley Museum and Library.)

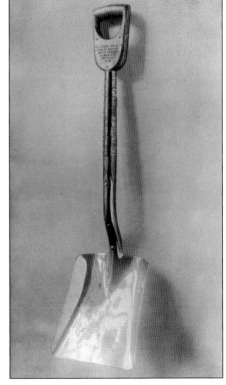

This ceremonial ground-breaking shovel was used at the dedication ceremony to represent the first dig of the Coleman DuPont Road near the Delaware-Maryland border on September 18, 1911. The shovel, as indicated by the number of attached plates below the handle, was used nine times, representing different sections of the original or assigned sections of the DuPont Highway. (Hagley Museum and Library.)

48

In this 1921 photograph, there are identical signs posted on the opposing concrete walls to mark the southern state line to Delaware, opposite Berlin, Maryland. The signs announce: "1 State, DuPont Road." The road did not receive its U.S. Route 113 moniker until 1925.

Ellendale Swamp is pictured during 1919. The first section of roadway was constructed in 1912. They were considered lighter sections of concrete than what was standard by 1929. While no immediate stress and wear was evident from the original construction, the heavy volume of traffic was a concern. Traffic counts taken in 1929 indicated that more traffic (50 percent) occurred on the Georgetown-to-Selbyville section than on the Georgetown-to-Milford section. Plans were prepared in 1930 to widen the Coleman DuPont Road south of Georgetown to Selbyville.

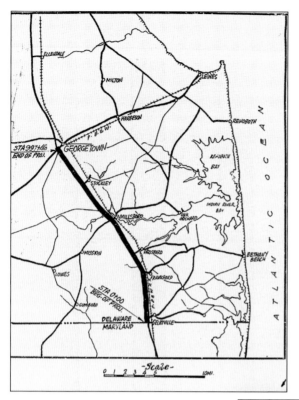

By 1930, the first original section of the Coleman DuPont Road was widened 4 feet under Contract 145 to accommodate traffic safety and preservation of the concrete roadway. During 1929 and into the early 1930s, Chief Engineer W. W. Mack stated that it was the policy of the department to widen highways as soon as the needs of traffic demonstrated its necessity. Many roads were widened and improved. However, the Coleman DuPont Road from Milford to Selbyville was only 14 feet in width. Excluding dirt and slag roads operated by the department, this section was the only through highway in the state that was less then 16 feet in width at the time. (DELDOT Archive Plans.)

This image is on the Coleman DuPont Road near Georgetown, the county seat of Sussex County since 1791. Georgetown holds an unusual event known as Return Day, meaning election returns. The town holds a day-long parade and festival two days after Election Day. It is a ritual held over from Colonial days when citizens would meet in front of the Georgetown Courthouse to hear the results of the election. The winning candidate rides in a carriage with the loser and the chairs of the county's political parties. They ceremonially "bury the hatchet" in a tub of sand.

Many of the early acquisitions by Coleman du Pont were outright acquisitions, particularly in the Ellendale area (as with Ellendale State Forest, shown here). Coleman du Pont envisioned some of the excess lands would become experimental areas for agricultural practices. The vision became relatively true. When the lands of the Coleman DuPont Road, Inc., were turned over to the new state highway department to administer in 1917, all the forested land acquired became property of DELDOT. Eventually the land was turned over to the Department of Agriculture and the state forestry department for management and for forestry purposes. Then again, in 1960, Frank V. du Pont (T. Coleman's son) provided to the state the last remaining stock in the Coleman DuPont Road, Inc. Over 542 acres of land representing the current and excess right-of-way along the U.S. 113 corridor from south of Milford to the Delaware-Maryland boarder were transferred to the State of Delaware. Included in the transfer were rentals and franchise agreements on different portions of land. (Department of Agriculture.)

By 1930, the state forestry department was developing tree nursery farms and experimental growing programs for the Ellendale State Forest. This rugged and natural timber sign was located along the Coleman DuPont Road five miles south of Milford and marks the entrance to the nursery facility. Saplings were grown in protected environments by the state forester in preparation for transplanting them throughout the state forest and throughout the state. (Department of Agriculture.)

The Coleman DuPont Road passed through a field of sweet potatoes in rural Sussex County in 1920. As early as 1868, Sussex County cultivated sweet potatoes, producing an annual yield of 100,000 bushels up to the year 1900. The crop would remain a viable industry until black rot, a root disease, struck in 1940.

Notice the whiter strip of road to the right on this span of road between Selbyville and Georgetown in 1931. To increase safety and reduce the number of head-on collisions, it was determined that portions of the original Coleman DuPont Road had to be widened. An additional 4 feet of concrete surface was laid. It should also be noted that the use of a white stripe to divide the north and southbound travel way was first seen on the DuPont Highway in 1917.

This view is north of Magnolia along the original corridor of the Coleman DuPont Road in 1936. Under the commission of Chief Engineer W. W. Mack, trees and natural beauty were preserved or enhanced where possible. Also, in many sections along the roadway, tree spraying for insect and disease control was not uncommon. Under Mack's authorization, improvement of the roadside by the sodding of slopes and banks and the planting and care of trees, shrubs, and flowers added much to the pleasure and interest of the motoring public.

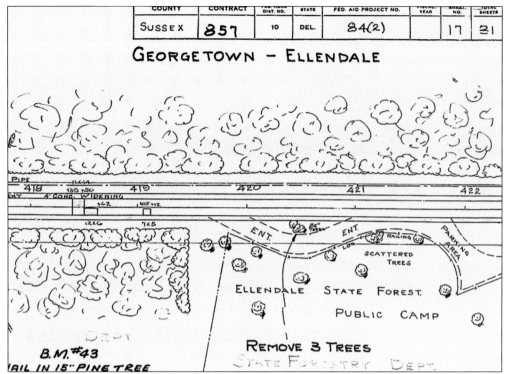

COUNTY	CONTRACT	FED. ROAD DIST. NO.	STATE	FED. AID PROJECT NO.	FISCAL YEAR	SHEET NO.	TOTAL SHEETS
SUSSEX	857	10	DEL.	84(2)		17	31

GEORGETOWN – ELLENDALE

ELLENDALE STATE FOREST
PUBLIC CAMP
REMOVE 3 TREES

B.M. #43
NAIL IN 15" PINE TREE

Beyond light construction projects administered by the state highway department, other federal programs to help relieve the Great Depression were also benefited by the department. A large amount of ditching had been undertaken to improve drainage along the state's highways, particularly in lower Kent County and throughout Sussex County. Secured by the WPA, the Civilian Conservation Corps (CCC) undertook routine maintenance—sealing cracks; patching the surface of various types of pavements; care for shoulders, ditches, culverts, and bridges; mowing and brambling right-of-way; trash collection; painting traffic lines; the repair and maintenance of traffic signals and warning signs; and planting, spraying, and caring for trees and shrubbery. More importantly, the CCC was a main force in creating and improving the Ellendale State Forest and many of its roads, research plantings, and early structures and buildings. The rest area along the DuPont Highway completed in 1939 is one of those CCC projects that benefited the DuPont Highway with roadside amenities. State Contract 857 in 1948 altered the front of the facility, but it remains relatively the same. (Above, DELDOT Archive Plans; below, Department of Agriculture.)

Magnolia is pictured looking south in 1934. Johnson General Store is on the right. Because a straight road already existed here, it was determined that the Coleman DuPont Road should be brought through town but only after securing the consent of town officials.

The Coleman DuPont Road on the approach to St. Georges in New Castle County is pictured looking north in 1930. Coleman du Pont had agreed to continue funding the construction of the original road after turning the project over to the Delaware Highway Department, but he did not contribute to the cost of the lift bridge that spanned the Chesapeake and Delaware Canal. Any bridge over the canal was the responsibility of the Chesapeake and Delaware Canal Company.

A 1926 photograph of the lift bridge at St. Georges shows the 260-foot-long steel structure that used opposing towers and pulleys as a counterweight to lift the roadbed and allow a ship to pass.

A close-up of the lift bridge over the canal at St. Georges in 1930 shows the gates up and a green light. Ships and boats on the approach to St. Georges were required to blow their horns loudly and clearly. From a control station, the bridge tenor mechanically lowered the gates and turned on the red signal light to stop any motorized traffic. The bridge platform then rose through a pulley system in the opposing towers.

The South Market Street Draw Bridge in Wilmington is seen looking north here in 1926. This was the north end of Coleman DuPont Road. Here it joined with an existing Wilmington city street. For the first time in Delaware history, the state had a paved surface road that connected all three county seats.

An older brick road with trolley tracks is evident in the foreground of this southward-looking 1926 image of the South Market Street Draw Bridge. This was considered a rundown and industrial section of town. In 1925, Chief Engineer C. D. Buck reported that in the state system of over 504 miles of highway, this section was the least attractive and most disgusting: "Since it is the first link in the boulevard through the State and one of the main gateways to Wilmington, it is surprising that no organized effort has been made to improve this street and bridge."

This is an artist's rendition of the Wilmington Causeway, DuPont Highway, and Route 13 over the Christina River and into the city of Wilmington. Two different renditions were prepared to enhance the South Wilmington area, but only one was selected. Work began on a new bridge known as the South Market Street Bridge or Riley Bridge in late 1925; it was completed in 1927. It was built by the Dravo Company and Pittsburgh and Bethlehem Steel Company for a combined $466,277.68. The construction exceeded its initial budget because of unsuitable foundations. The final cost was approximately $545,000, of which New Castle County Levy Court contributed $166,666.66.

Coleman DuPont Road crosses at Dover's Silver Lake in 1936. Silver Lake is a 167-acre man-made lake that drains into the upper St. Jones River at Dover. By 1936, a bypass east of Dover rerouted some of the through traffic, but this span was eventually widened. Expansion plans were prepared by the DELDOT's bridge engineers with assistance by E. William Martin, AIA, as a consulting architect. The bridge design called for brick veneer over reinforced concrete with white marble balustrades. The roadway provided four lanes of traffic with sidewalks on both sides. The combination of red brick and white marble resulted in a Georgian architecture that blended well with the Colonial atmosphere of Dover.

A 1923 directional and mileage road sign was posted along the Coleman DuPont Road at Georgetown. In 1929, the American Association of State Highway Officials (AASHO) in cooperation with the Bureau of Public Roads designated a system of signs for uniformly marking the highways in the United States. The improved "button type" standards were adopted by all states. Preexisting road and traffic signs delineating highways were soon replaced. This enabled travelers to recognize the signs on a uniform basis without having to learn new sign codes in each passing state.

On the Coleman DuPont Road south of Wilmington, note the Texaco motor oil billboard on the right. In 1925, it was first suggested that roadside advertising should be taxed to assist in defraying the maintenance cost for roads. In 1926, it was recommended 8¢ per square foot be levied on signs now erected within 200 feet of Delaware's state highways.

Coleman DuPont Road is pictured at Ellendale in 1923. The automobile is driving down the center of the road because some portions of the Coleman DuPont Road between Milford and Selbyville were only 14 feet in width, not wide enough to accommodate two-way traffic. W. W. Mack (1880–1966) was named chief engineer in 1929 and spent more years in that post than any individual in the history of the Delaware Highway Department. Mack supervised such projects as the dualizing of U.S. Route 13 and the widening of Philadelphia Pike. He led the department through the Great Depression and World War II, and he was principally responsible for promoting tourism by providing access to Delaware's beaches.

At Coleman DuPont Road and Shawnee Road in Sussex County in September 1923, note the early Texaco gas station on the right. Texaco began as the Texas Fuel Company in 1901 in Beaumont, Texas, and for many years was the only company selling gasoline in all 50 states. Buildings to the left belong to a chicken farm. Before the Coleman DuPont Road, raising chickens had been a minor business. With the completion of the road, and as a result of the innovations of the broiler industry, poultry farmers in the 1930s realized the enormous profit available in trucking broiler chickens to urban markets. Sussex County became the largest poultry-producing county in the United States, a distinction it still maintains.

This is Millsboro in 1936. Former chief engineer C. W. Buck concluded that with the state highway department nearing its completion of the Coleman DuPont Road, it was appropriate to make all Delaware roads an avenue of beauty—as much as cost would permit. Buck reported that the greatest care had been taken to make roads smooth, safe, and durable, but they could not be deemed finished until beautification projects were completed. A systematic program of tree planting commenced. During the early contracts, 1,000 young trees were planted along different highways, including the Coleman DuPont Road, with numbers being equally distributed among each county. The early stock included pine, red oak, and sugar maple.

Coleman DuPont Road at Little Heaven in Kent County is shown in the early 1930s. Little Heaven was a name applied to a group of cabins a local farmer, Jahue Reed, a former Delaware governor, built in the 1870s for Irish workers who labored in his orchards. A nearby community divided by a wetland crossing was referred to as "Little Hell." This other farming community has vanished but was believed to house African Americans families and workers in small cabins for either Reed's other agricultural holdings or for Thomas Henry's land. Little Heaven is a frequent Delaware entry in lists of odd American place names. Withstanding more contemporary times, the L. M. Webb Roadside Market (right) is a long-standing farm produce stand located near the Little Heaven area.

This is a 1941 photograph of U.S. Route 113 (Coleman DuPont Road) at the Rising Sun spur. Continuing straight, travelers drive into south Dover. Note the early Esso station on the left. Eastern States Standard Oil had been founded in 1911 and headquartered in Irving, Texas. Esso is an international trade name for Exxon Mobil and its related companies. The brand name has been replaced by Exxon in the United States. This section of the DuPont Highway is now known as State Route 10A and U.S. 113A.

Sussex County once had more forest and swampland than today. The Coleman DuPont Road, here near Ellendale, helped make Delaware the leading poultry producing state in the country. As the industry rose, timberland was cleared and swamps were filled in to make more acreage for chicken houses and crop cultivation necessary to support the birds. Small-town life in Sussex County improved with farmers having more income. The added cash was spent on tractors and trucks and a move to modernization, just as Coleman du Pont had envisioned.

A farmer's roadside produce stand sits between Magnolia and Rising Sun in Kent County in 1924. Roadside markets became common along the Coleman Dupont Road. In 1926, the state highway department petitioned that merchants who sold anything other than their own homegrown produce should be required to obtain a merchant's license.

Coleman DuPont Road runs alongside Barrett's Chapel and cemetery in Kent County in 1941. Philip Barratt built a church in 1780 between Little Heaven and Frederica, and it was here that believers decided in 1784 to organize the Methodist Episcopal Church. Hence it has been called "The Birthplace of Modern Methodism" and "The Cradle of Methodism in America." This photograph also illustrates a wider travel lane with a full dirt shoulder. "Hot-mix" or pavement was applied over the concrete road surface to preserve the base foundation from complete reconstruction.

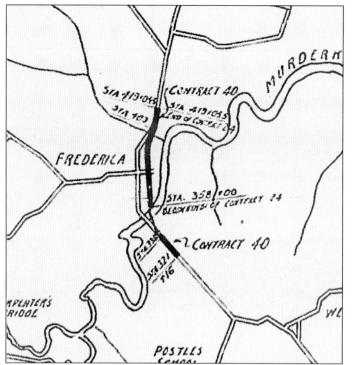

Contracts 24 A–D and Contract 40 included a new and reconstructed causeway through Frederica of 1.21 miles. It also included two new bridge crossings. Rather than going directly through Federica's only north-south road, the state highway department adhered to Coleman du Pont's approach by constructing a parallel road that tied into the mainline. One could argue that this may be the first bypass in Delaware, created in 1920. (DELDOT Archive Plans.)

Bridge 8F (Frederica Bridge, shown in 1928) was a steel girder bridge completed in 1920. Spanning the Murderkill River, it was one of the longest bridge crossings on the Coleman DuPont Road (excluding the Chesapeake and Delaware Canal). The bridge consists of four spans and presented an uncommon variant of the concrete-encased steel girders within its design. The bridge was also one of the first major bridge design projects developed by the state highway department during World War I. Significant repairs occurred some 80 years later, but the bridge is still in use and looks very similar to when it was first constructed.

McDonough in New Castle County is pictured in January 1924. The crossroads community located south of Boyds Corner was named for Thomas McDonough, who was born in Trap (McDonough), Delaware, on December 31, 1783. Thomas served in the U.S. Navy with distinction, particularly through the navy's infancy and during conflicts with France and then Great Britain during the War of 1812. He became master commandant in 1813 and was referred to as Commodore McDonough for the remainder of his life. His residence still exists as well, as a small cemetery plot where he and other family members of the McDonough community reside. (Hagley Museum and Library.)

Two cars on the Coleman DuPont Road approach a railroad crossing, looking south at Ellendale, in 1924. There was an alarming number of train and car collisions. In 1926, there were 63 at grade crossings, only 23 of which had a warning sign. In that year, there were 21 fatalities. The Delaware Highway Department, with the cooperation of the Pennsylvania Railroad, worked to eliminate grade crossings. Their efforts paid off. The following year, fatalities decreased to five. In 1928, the number was down to two.

In 1936, plans were made to eliminate the grade crossing on the South Market Street Causeway in Wilmington. The construction was completed in 1938 by J. A. Bader and Company for $206,685. Traffic had been detoured during construction by a temporary road. The bridge project was the second grade crossing elimination under the Federal Works Program, permanently eliminating the traffic hazard of crossing the high-speed rail line and time spent waiting for trains to pass. This location had been one of the most dangerous crossings designated in the state. The design of the bridge called for a reinforced concrete structure with two-way reinforced flat slabs, supported by reinforced "mushroom-like" concrete columns. The road width is 44 feet, and 5-foot sidewalks are present on each end. Federal funds paid for this structure with no cost to the state or railroad except for the right-of-way. Note the same Atlantic White Flash business on the left in both photographs and the "newly renovated" Hotel Olivere billboard on the right, advertising a room at $1.25, $2 with shower. The hotel was at Seventh and Shipley Streets.

This is the removal of the old bridge and creation of the new roadbed and bridge at Drawyers Creek in 1924. By 1931, the Drawyers and Appoquinimink Bridges in New Castle County formed a section of dual highway. Both bridges were bordered by marshes of poor subsoil to secure suitable foundations. Extensive fill was needed, and concrete pilings had to be driven approximately 75 feet deep. In September 1931, a 4.91-mile span of the dual highway between St. Georges and Drawyers opened to traffic. Grading was also completed to Fieldsboro, another 4.4 miles. By 1932, the dual DuPont Highway and Route 13 was complete to State Road (U.S. Route 40).

Drawyers Bridge is pictured in 1933 near Odessa. Less than 10 years after its construction and in preparation of the dual highway for the Dupont Highway to Dover, the Drawyers Bridge on the southbound road had to be repaired. Two piers and the south abutment settled approximately 30 inches. The repairs called for raising the entire superstructure of the settled spans by hydraulic jacks and filling the space between the piers and slabs with concrete. The contractors were Spencer, White, and Prentiss of New York, at a cost of $4,993. Along with the raising of the Drawyers Bridge, the roadbed macadam had to be replaced.

The easily spotted concrete strip of the Coleman DuPont Road passes Smyrna at New Street in January 1929. Smyrna was settled prior to the American Revolution on the south bank of Duck Creek and had had several names until the state assembly officially recognized it as Smyrna in 1806. The building on the right is believed to be the Wayside Inn, a long-standing restaurant.

Even current residents of Smyrna will recognize this stretch of the DuPont Highway as it enters town looking north. The streetscape hasn't changed much since the time of the photograph in the early 1930s and following the widening construction of a dual highway that occurred in 1934. Most median strips have since been paved, and trees aligning the Odd Fellows Cemetery have been removed.

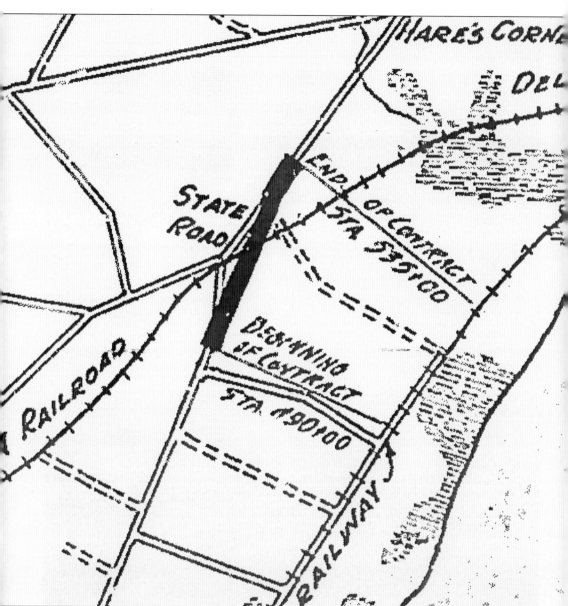

Many early state contracts reference the beginning or termination of their project limits at State Road just south of New Castle. This is also known as the convergence where U.S. 13 (DuPont Highway) and U.S. 40 (Pulaski Highway) interchange or meet. At the end of 1927, Chief Engineer C. D. Buck concluded that with the 40- and 38-foot widening of pavements on the Philadelphia Pike and the South Wilmington roadway corridor to State Road, an almost "perfect" highway was nearly completed. Suggested as the fastest, the safest, and the most desirable to travel, the DuPont Highway is a road of proper width built for traffic moving in only one direction and sufficiently far removed from other roads to prevent "night blinding" from headlights. To provide such a superhighway, Buck recommend that other segments of the Dupont Boulevard or Highway be widened or dualized beginning at State Road. As such, he offered to construct between St. Georges and State Road Station a 20-foot road paralleling the present highway at a distance of possibly 30 feet to the east or west of the current alignment. (DELDOT Archive Plans.)

The Coleman DuPont Road south of Wilmington is pictured looking south at State Road or U.S. Route 40 in 1924. The Coleman DuPont Road veers off to the left and runs beneath the railroad bridge that was dug out in an earlier photograph. This juncture is where the dual highway soon became a divided highway under State Contract 114 beginning in 1929.

The Route 13 and 40 interchange is now more recognizable to present Delaware drivers. By September 1934, the DuPont Highway and Route 13 had been expanded into a dual highway between Wilmington and Dover. U.S. Route 40 was also being dualized at this time to the Maryland state line, but it was not complete until later in the 1930s.

Coleman DuPont Road is seen looking south at Garrison Lake near Smyrna in 1923. Garrison Lake or Garrison Mill is an 86-acre state recreational area, popular for boating and fishing. It was also a section of road that required extensive fill for its foundation.

The Coleman DuPont Road at Red Lion in New Castle County is seen prior to dualizing. Red Lion is named for the Red Lion Creek, a name left over from Red Lion Hundred. "Hundreds" were once used for the basis of representation in Delaware's General Assembly but now have no political significance. This section of the DuPont Highway was first improved under State Contracts 33 and 33A (bridge) that included improvements from St. Georges to Tybout's Corner in 1922–1923. This section was ultimately the first dualized section, beginning in the early 1930s from State Road to St. Georges under State Contract 114.

Route 113, Coleman DuPont Road, is seen in Sussex County during the 1930s. Note the newer, additional strip of pavement to the left and the white line shifted from the road's original center. In 1917, a section of road near Selbyville became the first in the United States to use a white center line.

Coleman DuPont Road near Georgetown was resurfaced in 1931 with a 2-inch course of amiesite and an additional concrete shoulder on both sides. In 1930, some 19 miles of widening took place on the Coleman DuPont Road between Selbyville and Georgetown. Although earlier recommendations called for a uniform 20-foot width, the total width of the roadway became 18 feet. The road segment was first built in 1915 and 1916 before the inception of the state highway department.

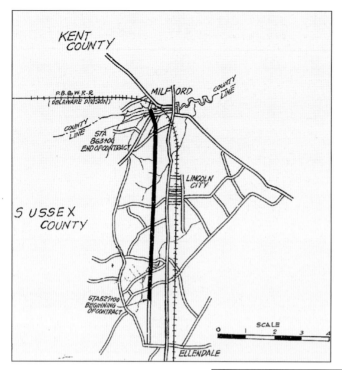

State Highway Department Contract 8 continued where the Coleman DuPont Road, Inc., left off. In 1918, the state adhered to the survey lines and designs already laid out by the Coleman DuPont Road Company. While Coleman du Pont's original scheme called for a 200-foot right-of-way, highway engineers and right-of-way officials selected a 60-foot width for sufficient needs of a single highway in this location. State Contract 173 in 1931 resulted in an additional 4 feet of widening in this area because of safety. Ultimately, in 1992, this segment of roadway was finally dualized with a grassy median between Milford and Georgetown. (DELDOT Archive Plans.)

Two cars pass each other on the Coleman DuPont Road near Milford in 1920. Milford is located on the border between Kent and Sussex Counties. The Kent County portion was settled in 1680 by Henry Bowan on Saw Mill Range. A century later, the Reverend Sydenham Thorne built a dam across the Mispillion River to generate power for his gristmill and sawmill. The city was incorporated February 5, 1807. Traffic issues are now becoming a concern within the Milford area. Plans for a bypass corridor either west or east or expanding the existing U.S. 113 alignment were not well received by residents of Milford and Lincoln in 2006.

This demonstration area is on lands belonging to M. C. Whitehead in August 1939. The view is of the east side of the Coleman DuPont Road about a half-mile south of the Lincoln crossroads. The sign reads "Demonstration Area Thinning Pruning Fire Hazard Reduction made by C C C Camp S53 under supervision of the State Forestry Department 1938." Throughout the mid- to late 1930s, the Civilian Conservation Corps employed individuals, some high school dropouts and young professionals down and out, to undertake manual labor positions involved with public works. The CCC in Delaware is credited for developing the Ellendale State Forest's infrastructure while also improving the surrounding area, clearing out dead branches and thinning out species of trees that did not conform to the state forester's replanting and silver culture operations. During any significant dry periods, an errant cigarette could have caused a major fire along U.S. 113. Thinning and pruning was essential. (Department of Agriculture.)

Taken from the Coleman DuPont Road two miles south of the Lincoln crossroads, the October 1929 view of the State Forest Tree Nursery shows beds of transplants from the southeast corner of the nursery. Today this is a dense area of pine forests. (Department of Agriculture.)

The road crosses at the Mispillion River. In 1926, an improved highway east of Milford intended to connect the Coleman DuPont Road with the Milford-Rehoboth highway was surveyed. The bypass fell under federal financial assistance since it provided Milford with the most effective way to reduce summer beach traffic in downtown Milford and it relieved portions of traffic on the Coleman DuPont Road through Milford. A section of the engineering plan is illustrated from State Contracts 104A and 104B as well as a photograph taken in 1931. The bridge still exists today and is still operable as a Scherzer rolling lift bascule bridge designed by Keller and Harrington from Chicago. (Above, Delaware State Archives; below, DELDOT Archive Plans.)

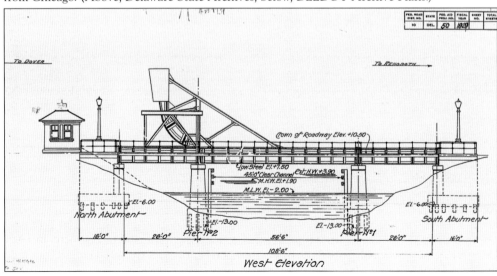

Coleman DuPont Road is shown at the intersection of Route 28 in Georgetown in the early 1930s. Route 28 is the present U.S. 9 or County Seat Highway that connects Georgetown with the town of Laurel on the west and Georgetown with Lewes on the east. U.S. 9 is one of Sussex County's primary east-west routes. The Atlantic Service Station at the northeast intersection corner offered gas at 15¢ a gallon.

A car is at the intersection of the Coleman DuPont Road and Laurel Crossroads in 1923 near Georgetown. As automobile ownership increased, so too did government involvement. In 1905, Delaware's general assembly passed the first registration laws and set the speed limit at "one mile in three minutes." Two years later, driver's licenses were initially issued.

Coleman DuPont Road heads north on the approach to St. Georges in 1922. The lift bridge is not yet constructed. Prior bridges over the Chesapeake and Delaware Canal had included a swing bridge when the canal had locks. The bridge was removed with the locks when the canal was widened and deepened to sea level. St. Georges is named after a creek that flowed in the area prior to the canal. Notice the cut slopes have no ground cover and are susceptible to erosion. Many contracts that the highway department administered involved the use of sodding to combat that problem.

Shown here is Coleman DuPont Road on the north side of St. Georges in 1930. The lift bridge designed and built by the U.S. Army Corps of Engineers was in full view. The Chesapeake and Delaware Canal is a 14-mile-long, 450-foot-wide, and 35-foot-deep shipping lane that cuts across New Castle County and reduces the journey from Philadelphia to Baltimore by 300 nautical miles. The idea of a canal here began as early as the mid-1700s. The canal first opened in 1829. The state highway department was responsible for securing any right-of-way necessary for the bridge and approach roadway.

The Coleman DuPont Road shows an actual curve in this photograph taken November 27, 1922. This location is just south of Tybout's Corner. In the far background, the Newark and Delaware City Railroad crossing is evident by Corbit Station. The farms of Clarence Clayton and Mrs. Preston Lea abut the road.

Coleman DuPont Road at Rogers Corner south of Wilmington is seen looking north in the 1920s. Rogers Corner divides two main transportation gateways into south Wilmington. The area where the photographer stood is where the current Interstate 495 crosses over the U.S. 13 DuPont Highway. This photograph was also taken shortly after State Contract 82, which concerned the portion of highway between State Road and Wilmington Causeway, was completed in 1928. Work consisted of 20 feet of concrete widening. Upon completion, it was reported that the 38 feet of total pavement width does not always function as a dual roadway since some drivers persist on holding to the center of the road instead of driving to the right as typically required.

Two cars are on the Coleman DuPont Road near Odessa in September 1923. Early motorists were taught to drive by car salesmen, automobile associations, athletic clubs like the YMCA, or by family and friends. Not until the 1930s did high schools offer driver education.

This is an original Coleman DuPont Road seal or title sheet logo for Contract RM 7, Odessa to St. Georges. The contract was never undertaken by Coleman du Pont's corporation, but a simple center line was developed, as well as cross sections. State Contracts 28, 32, and 37—built during the early 1920s—undertook the transportation effort, which included a new bridge at Drawyers Creek. (DELDOT Archive Plans.)

A perfectly straight stretch of the Coleman DuPont Road goes through the Ellendale forest. There was no curb, no drainage system, no paved shoulder for road emergencies, and, more incidentally, no traffic.

This lone car rides in 1920 on an elevated roadbed built through the Ellendale Swamp. The Ellendale Swamp once had a notorious reputation as a hideaway for criminals during the Colonial period and as a favorite refuge for loyalists during the American Revolution.

Philadelphia Pike, looking south toward Wilmington in 1923, was not officially part of the Coleman DuPont Road but would become incorporated into U.S. Route 13 from Wilmington north to the Pennsylvania state line, completing the DuPont Highway the full length of the state. What is also important to highlight is the continued use of wire fencing along the edge of right-of-ways and typically along agricultural fields. As a means to reduce accidents at crossroads and at railroad crossings, the highway department had the authority to replace corner hedges at such points with open fences. In addition, the department would enter a lease with the property owner to not allow seasonal crops such as corn or other vegetation at intersection corners that would impair the view. Such declarations were considered duties of the highway department equal to repairs of the highway itself.

Providing alternative routes for Route 13 and DuPont Highway to areas north was the new Governor Printz Boulevard or Industrial Highway in April 1935, here looking north. The DuPont Company's chemical plant at Edgemoor is in the distance and is still in operation. The modern highway, I-495, now runs between the Governor Printz and the DuPont facility. Governor Printz Boulevard also provided alternative access to steel and other industries located farther north and northeast of Wilmington.

Route 13 and Philadelphia Pike in Claymont are pictured in 1929. The billboard on the left is an advertisement for a car dealership, announcing new Cadillacs, LaSalles, and Fleetwoods for sale. The first car manufacturers were bicycle and carriage makers. Hundreds of new auto companies hit the market between 1900 and 1910. By the 1930s, most manufacturers had gone out of business. Ford, General Motors, and Chrysler emerged as the leading suppliers thanks to mass marketing, annual model change, advertising, and product appeal. Philadelphia Pike was also the first corridor connection in Delaware to be widened.

A lonely stretch of road in New Castle County is pictured looking south between St. Georges and Odessa in 1922. Once a motorist ventured south of the canal, there was open road and little habitation until Dover. The Coleman DuPont Road, the dual DuPont Highway, and especially the newer Route 1 have brought a building and population boom to lower Delaware.

State Police Station No. 2 is pictured near Route 13, DuPont Highway, and Route 40 around 1930. By 1925, there were 35 men serving as state police officers at five stations located off the Coleman DuPont Road corridor. One of their initial duties was protecting the highway against overloaded trucks. In 1924, they had 17,217 trucks weighed. Like today, the officers made arrests for motor vehicle violations, criminal behavior, and documented vehicular accidents.

State Contract 1 included a 4.05-mile stretch from Cheswold (Bishops Corner) to Dover. Construction consisted of a combination of concrete and macadam roadway surfaces and was completed in the early 1920s. This segment of the Coleman DuPont Road led to downtown Dover, where portions of the roadway were already improved. One of the main goals for the state highway department under Coleman du Pont was establishing the foundation for Dover as the main or central political and transportation hub for the state. All north-south routes, including the DuPont Highway, must pass through Dover. (DELDOT Archive Plans.)

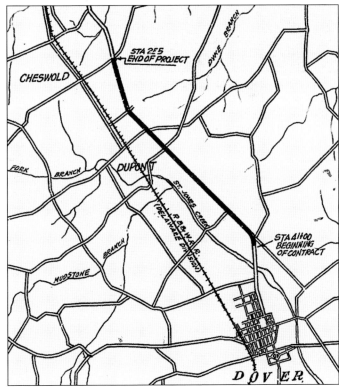

In some places, summer heat caused expansion in the concrete that had not been properly estimated and resulted in "blow ups" of the road, like this section near Selbyville in 1919. This was one of many lessons learned in the early construction of concrete roads.

Another blow up is shown here in Sussex County in 1919. This damaged section of Coleman DuPont Road had to be lifted away by truck and chain so a new section could be built. Road repair, as well as road construction, was in its infancy, so it was learn as you go.

Shown is an original Coleman DuPont Road seal or title sheet logo for Contract RM 6, Smyrna to Odessa. The contract was never undertaken by the DuPont corporation, but a simple center line with a very rudimentary survey was developed. State Contracts 25A, 27, and 28, built during the early 1920s, undertook the transportation effort, which included new bridges at Blackbird and Appoquinimink Creeks. (DELDOT Archive Plans.)

The Coleman DuPont Road ran north of Odessa near Drawyers Creek in 1931. This area was not yet dualized, but change was on the way. In 1927, the chief engineer of the Delaware Highway Department, C. Douglass Buck, recommended in the annual report that the Coleman Dupont Road be widened or dualized: "A 20-foot road should parallel the present highway at a distance of 30 feet to the east or west of the current alignment." The divided highway was born.

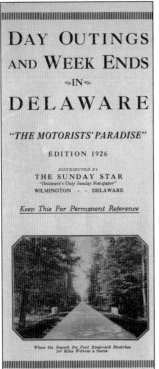

A travel pamphlet published in 1926 by the Wilmington *Sunday Star*, Delaware's "only Sunday newspaper," calls Delaware a motorists' paradise. The caption below the photograph reads, "Where the Superb DuPont Boulevard Stretches for Miles Without a Curve."

Three

FIRST DIVIDED HIGHWAY

The DuPont Highway and Route 13 are viewed looking north into Smyrna during the 1930s. A sign just beyond a row of trees welcomes motorists. The row of trees and fencing are gone now, but present area residents will still recognize the cemetery behind the trees and the entrance to Main Street that angles off to the left.

An army of workers is ready to build the dual section of the DuPont Highway. Construction began at a critical time because the nation was enduring the Great Depression, the largest economic downturn in history. The Great Depression had originated in the United States with the stock market crash on October 29, 1929. In 1932, it was estimated that over 600 individuals were put to work on Delaware's roadways. In 1931–1934, the federal government added a considerable sum of money to provide additional work relief through the Civil Works Administration. Roadwork offered one of the best opportunities to employ a large workforce. Under the supervision and administration of the Delaware Highway Department, more than 1,400 people were employed on CWA projects. In 1931, the department first undertook an emergency program under State Contract 209. The highway work intended to improve employment conditions, particularly in the vicinity of Wilmington. The program entailed a large amount of rush work, such as grading. Both photographs are near Hares Corner.

Excavation work is performed on the dual section of the DuPont Highway near Drawyers Church in 1931. In early September 1931, another 4.91-mile section of the dual highway extending from St. Georges to Drawyers was open to traffic. Grading was also completed to Fieldsboro, another 4.4 miles. By 1932, the dual highway would be complete and operable from State Road (U.S. 40) to one mile south of Blackbird. Old Drawyers Presbyterian Church is in the far background of this photograph. Services began in the existing building in 1773 and continued until a new church was erected in Odessa in 1861. Many Colonial and state leaders are interred in the Old Drawyers cemetery.

A worker uses a trowel to apply the final touches to an additional lane on the DuPont Highway. It was painstaking, backbreaking, and knee-hurting work, but any job was appreciated during the 1930s. Many CWA projects directly involved sidewalks, clearing, and larger grading projects. Other skilled and semi-skilled workers were also needed, particularly for the dualizing projects for the DuPont Highway.

The state highway department advocated that Delaware's highway should be more than a strip of concrete. They championed not only the planting of trees and gardens along the route but information kiosks that would provide travelers with tourist information and advertise local businesses and events.

Because of their marshy conditions, both the Drawyers Creek and Appoquinimink Creek Bridges were difficult dual contracts to complete. Both twin concrete bridges were intended to match and resemble each other. However, they were both subcontracted out. Extra time and delay occurred because it was necessary to allow for proper settlement. The southbound bridge at Drawyers settled because of construction efforts on the northbound bridge. The new construction was in close proximity, so vibration, additional loads, and additional alteration of the subsurface caused the existing bridge at Drawyers to settle. As soon as the new northbound bridge was complete, the existing southbound bridge had to be significantly repaired. (DELDOT Archive Plans.)

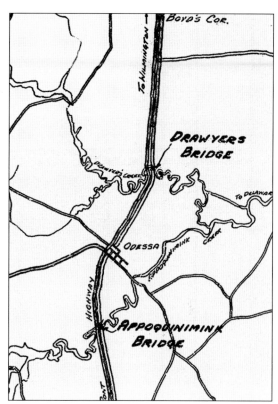

Here is the building of the matching bridge over the Appoquinimink River for the dual highway near Odessa in 1931. Odessa was founded as Cantwell's Bridge in 1731 after Capt. Edmund Cantwell's son Robert established a toll bridge over the river. The area prospered as a grain-shipping river port until the railroad came to Middletown. Farm produce soon went to Middletown for shipment, and Cantwell's Bridge, in a last-ditch effort to save itself, changed its name in 1855 to Odessa after a Ukrainian grain-shipping port of the same name.

Pictured here is the rural Blackbird Hill in New Castle County as seen in 1908. Blackbird Hill became part of the route for the two-lane Coleman DuPont Road. By 1934, it had become part of the divided highway. Blackbird Creek flows underneath the bridges pictured in both photographs. Both bridges were designed with vernacular art deco elements, which was common at the time but rare today. Nearby is Blackbird State Forest, a recreational area and Delaware's northernmost state forest, covering over 4,800 acres.

Workers create the dual highway north of St. Georges in 1929. The lift bridge is visible on the extreme left of the photograph. The dual highway, as the first divided highway under State Contract 114, stretched 7.67 miles between St. Georges and State Road.

The DuPont Highway and Route 13 are one mile north of St. Georges in 1933 by Red Lion Creek. Another federal program that helped employ people during the Great Depression was the Civilian Conservation Corps. Workers were assigned routine maintenance, such as patching and sealing cracks in the road, painting lines, repairing traffic signals, digging ditches, planting, mowing, and landscaping.

This is south of Blackbird in 1932. As each section of the DuPont Highway expanded into four lanes and another section awaited its turn, new signs were needed to alert motorists they were approaching or leaving a dual highway segment. The sign reads "Dual Highway–One Way," and its arrow directs motorists accordingly. There are two men behind the sign attaching it to the posts while one man watches. Some things never change.

Motorists on the DuPont Highway were alerted when the divided highway started. In this picture from 1933, they were alerted to when the divided highway ended. The practical application of a dual highway had established Delaware as the forerunner in this type of road construction. Highway department staff from around the world came to Delaware to see and learn.

The dual highway and State Police Station No. 3 are shown in Dover in 1934, before and after it became operational. The building was best known as the Delaware Building at the Sesquicentennial Exposition in Philadelphia. To commemorate the 150th anniversary of the signing of the Declaration of Independence, the Sesquicentennial International Exposition was held in Philadelphia from June 1 to December 1, 1926. The building's central room was 56 feet long and 30 feet wide, with a ceiling 16 feet high. The building was dedicated at the exposition on May 29, 1926, by Delaware governor Robert P. Robinson. After the exposition, the building was dismantled and reconstructed at Dover near the present site of the Dover Mall. The building was used until about 1958.

The DuPont Highway at Cheswold is shown north of Dover in 1934. The grassy median has yet to receive "improvements," such as trees and gardens, but it does have several crossovers for travelers who need to turn around. The original Coleman DuPont Road is obviously the lanes on the left. State Contract 286 from Dover to Bishops Corner was the last of the six dual-highway contract efforts the state highway department completed before Labor Day 1934.

Notice the row of trees near Biddles Corner in August 1931. Many planting contracts received the generous support of various individuals and community and civic clubs. Notably, Francis V. du Pont, the chairman of the highway department at this time, donated a large number of trees, which were planted during the fall of 1932 between Blackbird and State Road (U.S. 40). State forester W. S. Taber was also instrumental in fulfilling many of the highway department's planting contracts.

Shown here is Route 13 and DuPont Highway near the Old Union Methodist Church, a mile north of Blackbird. Levi Scott, a native of the area, became the first Delawarean to serve as a Methodist bishop.

This picture shows the approach to Smyrna from the south in 1934 near Belmont Hall. In September of that year, the final section of the dual highway between Wilmington and Dover opened to traffic. This completed a six-year program to unite Dover with the state's largest city, Wilmington.
The 46 miles between Wilmington and Dover were now considered a speedy and comfortable ride.

Smyrna at the Lake Como Bridge is pictured in 1934. Similar to the Blackbird Creek Bridges, the structures after the Lake Como spillway incorporate the art deco look in their design. The twin bridge was added in 1933–1934 under State Contract 285. Both bridges were later rebuilt with a ridged frame in 1940. Work also consisted of 46 to 66 feet of concrete dual widening. The contract was awarded to W. W. Truitt, Lincoln City, Delaware, at a cost of $161,269.50.

An aerial shot of the DuPont Highway just south of Wilmington at Rogers Corner was taken on April 23, 1933, as was the matching ground shot of the same billboard-plagued stretch of highway. Today Interstate 495 and its juncture with U.S. 13 would be seen.

Smyrna is pictured in the snow looking south in 1935. The Delaware Highway Department assumed the task of removing snow from roads. They used trucks and tractors equipped with front plows for the job and, in some cases, men with shovels.

Snow removal occurs on the Coleman DuPont Road in 1927 near Route 13 and State Road (Route 40). The billboard advertises a trip to Atlantic City, New Jersey, via the Wilmington-Pennsgrove Ferry for 50¢. Any traveler reading that billboard during such a wintry scene would think not of casinos but of summer fun at the Atlantic City boardwalk and beaches.

U.S. 40 is viewed looking north toward U.S. 13 in the late 1920s. This juncture would ultimately be improved since it is the location where both dual roads meet. State Police Station No. 2 at State Road can be seen in the far background.

Pictured is the DuPont Highway south of Wilmington in 1931. The billboard (center) is advertising AC oil filters and spark plugs. AC Spark Plug Company was founded in 1908 by Frenchman Albert Champion, and General Motors purchased the firm a year later. The company added aircraft spark plugs to their Flint, Michigan, factory in 1916 and produced 50,000 plugs a day during World War I.

Now a very congested and developed area in Dover, here is how the junction of U.S. Routes 13 and 113 appeared in 1935. Note the billboard-size directional sign for motorists made by the state highway department. Just as today, popular destinations were Rehoboth and Delaware's other beaches. U.S. Route 13 and the DuPont Highway didn't take vacationers directly to the sand and sun, but it was the main route for most of the journey south.

Pictured is North Street to Silver Lake, Dover, in the early 1930s. The Esso gas station is located after the Silver Lake Bridge before entering or leaving Dover. Even though a single-lane bypass road was constructed in the early 1930s to circumnavigate around Dover to Little Heaven, this segment also served as part of the DuPont Highway as a direct link to Dover. Before "filling stations" existed, people bought gasoline from a barrel at the grocer or the hardware store. The increasing influence of the automobile in American society prompted the new business of gas stations, not only for fuel but auto repair. By 1930, Americans were using over 15 billion gallons of gasoline per year, and by 1935, there were over 200,000 gas stations in the United States.

The completed dual highway at Garrison Lake is pictured looking south in 1934. Notice how flat the southbound lanes (right) are at the curve in the road and at the bridge. By 1940, this section of the southbound lanes was replaced by an elevated curved surface to promote safety after a high number of accidents occurred. In the reconstruction photograph, looking north, the dwelling in the upper right still exists.

The DuPont Highway is seen looks north here between Tybout's Corner and Wrangle Hill in New Castle County after resurfacing was completed in 1938. Wrangle Hill was named after two families who had settled here and had a long-standing feud.

The new northbound bridge at Odessa on the dual highway is shown in 1932. Under the bridge project, efforts included hot-mix paving instead of the establishment of a thicker and heavier concrete approach road because of unstable subsurfaces. Soon after, the southbound adjacent bridge would settle and need emergency repair.

Pictured here facing south in 1933 is the DuPont Highway at Hares Corner with its intersection at Route 273, now one of the busiest intersections in the state. Note the four-sided, red-yellow-green traffic signal hanging above the road. The initial use of a four-sided traffic control device with three lights per side was at Woodward Avenue and Fort Street in Detroit, Michigan, in 1920. Semaphore traffic control devices were first used in 1908 and did little more than flash the words "Stop" and "Go." Traffic lights developed from the same concept as lights used in signaling train operators.

Rogers Corner, south of Wilmington, is seen at night in 1938. The lights were installed by Olivere Paving Company of Wilmington at a cost of $5,587. This was one of the first contracts ever advertised for increased visibility at night. Rogers Corner provided a significant choice for entering or leaving the city of Wilmington as areas south of the city limits were being developed to be some of the earliest suburbs.

St. Georges is pictured in 1930. Chief Engineer W. W. Mack said the dual highway would also attract tourists from other states. As such, Mack and the state highway department continued the dual highway design by opening bids on December 16, 1930, for another section of highway extending 4.91 miles in length from St. Georges to Drawyers Creek. Mack concluded that the completion of such a highway would be an outstanding achievement in highway construction, equaling the completion of the Coleman DuPont Road.

Route 13 and Philadelphia Pike are shown in 1937. Considered part of the Dupont Highway, it was one of the first corridors to be widened. In 1927, rights-of-way were obtained for additional land for widening use. This stretch of highway provided an example of the importance of securing ample rights-of-way when roads are first constructed. The widening of the Philadelphia Pike to an 80-foot right-of-way necessitated the acquisition of additional land on 34 properties, 33 secured by agreement and one by condemnation.

Farnhurst, a facility for mental illness south of Wilmington, is pictured in 1915 before the construction of the Coleman DuPont Road. The existing gravel road was incorporated into the thoroughfare. The aerial view, taken in 1933, is of the DuPont Highway passing in front of Farnhurst, now called the Delaware State Hospital. Farnhurst treats patients suffering from severe and persistent mental illness and nervous disorders. In the late 1800s, the New Castle County Trustees of the Poor had erected a facility to house the insane persons of the county, but in 1889, the state legislature directed the New Castle facility to be used for the benefit of all of Delaware. (Both Hagley Museum and Library.)

In 1932, the additional lanes for the DuPont Highway were constructed in front of Farnhurst, the Delaware State Hospital. In 1926, the Delaware Highway Department's chief engineer, C. Douglass Buck, had estimated that the volume of traffic passing Farnhurst far exceeded the amount of volume on any other road in the state. The bridge was part of the trolley line overpass.

According to the 1920 census, 223,000 people lived in Delaware, almost half in Wilmington. The DuPont Highway made it easier for people and businesses to relocate from the city. Population shifts spurred new housing construction and schools. It also meant there was a need for new cemeteries. This aerial shot shows Gracelawn Memorial Park, south of Wilmington and along the DuPont Highway, before it was "occupied" in 1933. (Hagley Museum and Library.)

Pictured is the road from Bishops Corner to Smyrna looking north in 1935. Note the bus. Fageol Motors of Oakland, California, in 1921 was the first company to manufacture a "Safety Bus." Earlier buses had been prone to tipping when cornering. The Fageol Safety Bus had a wider base and was built lower to the ground for ease of handling and passenger safety.

Shown in 1932 is the area north of Smyrna. Within the Smyrna area, medians transitioned into an urban median section to minimize right-of-way impacts to homes and business within the corridor. Note the roadside trees planted as part of the shoulder. Today those trees would be considered in the clear zone and removed.

This is a typical scene along the DuPont Highway heading toward Hares Corner by McCoy's Hill. Concrete drainage channels directed runoff directly into streams. This is hazardous for water quality and in the control of flash flooding. Today roadside runoff is directed into storm-water management ponds.

The DuPont Highway was never really finished. There were always "improvements," from landscaping and repairs to widening projects and resurfacing. In 1938, a 3.4-mile section of road between Tybout's Corner and Wrangle Hill in New Castle County was widened by 4 feet and resurfaced, a portion of which is shown here. The contractor was Wilson Construction Company of New Castle, and it cost $73,368. No sooner were the dual lands added to accommodate the northbound travel way than the existing travel surfaces on the southbound had to be reconstructed because of wear.

Route 13 south of Corbit Station in New Castle County is shown in the 1930s. The area got its name from a popular 18th-century tavern. Not all of Delaware's unusual place names come from old taverns, but colonists were said to have consumed about two gallons of brew as a daily dietary staple.

In 1938, the road is pictured north of Corbit, looking north to Tybout's Corner. The resurfacing and rebuilding of the south lane of the DuPont Highway from Wrangle Hill to Tybout's Corner replaced a roadway of nearly 20 years' use. In the reconstruction, the pavement was widened and the curve at Corbit was superelevated.

The resurfacing and rebuilding of the south lane of the DuPont Highway at Blackbird occurred in the late 1930s. After nearly 20 years of use, the road had been deemed rough and unserviceable. Hot-mix overlays smoothed the surface wear, which was beneficial to preserve both the base and vehicular tires. This section of the roadway, like others, was closely monitored in order to determine whether the application of asphalt would be economical for secondary roads.

This 1931 aerial view shows the DuPont Highway as a two-lane road through South St. Georges, not to be confused with St. Georges. South St. Georges is a smaller town on the south side of the canal, opposite its more populous neighbor. About a mile south of town, the DuPont Highway splits into a divided roadway and continues so onto Dover. The ground-level photograph shows the point of separation.

This is an aerial shot of the highway north of St. Georges approaching Tybout's Corner in 1931. This section of the dual highway was left in place or partially removed because of the recent construction of State Route 1.

On January 8, 1929, the department received bids for the construction of a dual highway from State Road to St. Georges under State Contract 114. The work was awarded to Old Line Construction from Chestertown, Maryland. The state highway department indicated that the dual highway would be a two-lane concrete road paralleling 50 feet of the present road. Chief Engineer C. D. Buck stated, "One way of traffic will be maintained on these two thoroughfares and it is hoped that greater safety will be secured, through the elimination of head-light glare and the possibility of head-on collisions. The completion of this project will afford an opportunity of testing the relative advantages of the two methods of handling heavy traffic." He would later coin the phrase that the dual highway design was "fool proof" from a safety perspective. Below is an image of the area north of Corbit Station in March 14, 1930, looking toward Red Lion. This photograph illustrates the successful completion of the first dual highway segment originating from this contract.

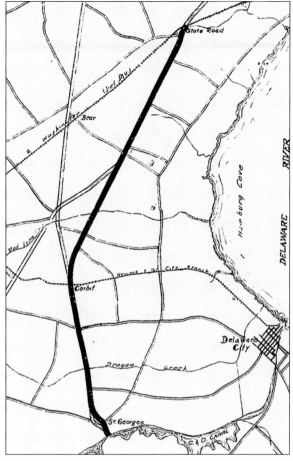

NORTH OF BASIN ROAD.
DUAL HIGHWAY.
DEL. STATE HIGHWAY DEP'T.
9-4-1933.

Shown here is the road north of Basin Road in 1933 near New Castle, with the typical traffic volume from commuters and other travelers. The current interchange of State Route 141 and Interstate 295 was later constructed within this area, which required a total overhaul and rerouting of Route 141 and its interchange with the DuPont Highway.

On August 22, 23, and 24, 1933, Delaware was inundated by rain and wind from the Chesapeake-Potomac Hurricane. Nearly 11.5 inches of rain fell, causing extensive flooding and property damage but no deaths. Trees fell, and roads and bridges were washed away. Traffic was suspended, and several towns were marooned for days. Hardest hit were portions near Smyrna at Garrisons Mill.

On September 1, 1940, flooding rains occurred near Smyrna. The Smyrna storm washed out three milldams in the vicinity, including the dam at Lake Como on the DuPont Highway. Waters overtopped and washed out the dam and roadway. A temporary bridge was placed in service within 72 hours. Ultimately, a new bridge with a ridged frame was placed with a span of 40 feet.

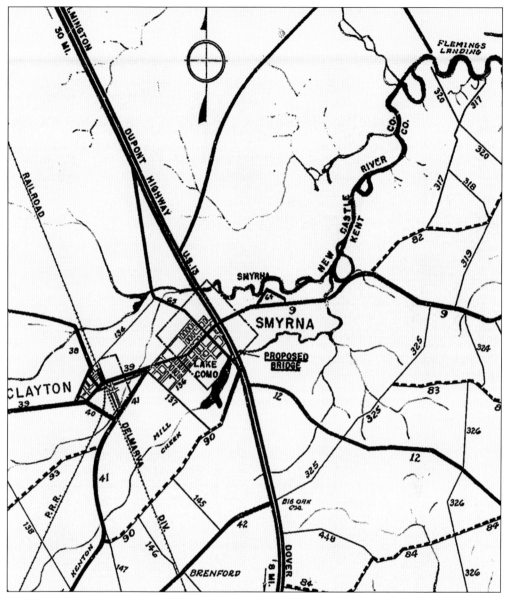

Contract 281A by Lake Como was quickly awarded because of washouts of the Smyrna Bridges at Lake Como. The bridges were replaced with a ridged frame to minimize a future washout occurrence. The southbound bridge still exists today but in poor condition. (DELDOT Archive Plans.)

This aerial view of St. Georges and the Dupont Highway was taken on September 11, 1930. At the bottom of the photograph is the original lift bridge that crossed the canal. The Chesapeake and Delaware Canal cuts across New Castle County and has inspired citizens of Delaware to refer to themselves as living "above the canal" or "below the canal," also referred to by some as "slower Delaware."

The 6,000-ton German freighter *Waukegan* was unable to stop when it lost power on approach to the lift bridge in St. Georges in November 1939. The *Waukegan* struck the south tower and destroyed the bridge. Two people were killed: the bridge operator and a sailor on the bridge.

Capt. Lloyd Reynolds blamed the accident on "unexpected currents of strength and direction" when called to testify at a Maritime Commission board of inquiry held to investigate the incident. The captain claimed the ship was traveling at 9 knots and blew its horn for the bridge to rise at 1,200 feet away. Then the ship lurched to starboard and all efforts to stop it failed.

A view shows the mangled steel after the *Waukegan* collided with the lift bridge. The loss of the bridge caused drivers great inconvenience. A detour road was built to Lums Pond to link motorists with the Summit Bridge, but only after rights-of-way were secured so the detour road could be constructed. Several properties were bought and some homes moved to new locations.

An aerial view shows St. Georges, the Chesapeake and Delaware Canal, and the St. Georges's Bridge, built by the Army Corps of Engineers and opened in 1942 to replace the lift bridge. With the opening of the Senator William Roth Bridge on State Route 1 in 1995 (not pictured), the Army Corps of Engineers favored removal of the St. Georges's Bridge. Local residents and the highway department, however, opposed the idea, so it remains. Also in view, to the left of the St. Georges's Bridge, is the original path of the Coleman DuPont Road and the empty space where the lift bridge once stood.

BIBLIOGRAPHY

Delaware's Historic Bridges: Survey and Evaluation of Historic Bridges with Historic Contexts for Highways and Railroads. Paramus, New Jersey: Lichtenstein Consulting Engineers, Inc., 2000.

Hoffecker, Carol. *Democracy in Delaware.* Wilmington, DE: Cedar Tree Books, 2004.

Mack, Warren W. "A History of Motor Highways in Delaware." *Delaware, A History of the First State.* H. Clay Reed, ed. New York: Lewis Historical Publishing Company, Inc., 1947.

National Register of Historic Places Registration Form for Ellendale State Forest Picnic Facility.

Rae, John. "Coleman du Pont and His Road." *Delaware History* v. 16 (Spring-Summer, 1975): 171–183.

State Highway Department Annual Reports, 1924–1940. Dover, DE.

www.arcadiapublishing.com

Discover books about the town where you grew up, the cities where your friends and families live, the town where your parents met, or even that retirement spot you've been dreaming about. Our Web site provides history lovers with exclusive deals, advanced notification about new titles, e-mail alerts of author events, and much more.

MADE IN THE USA

Arcadia Publishing, the leading local history publisher in the United States, is committed to making history accessible and meaningful through publishing books that celebrate and preserve the heritage of America's people and places. Consistent with our mission to preserve history on a local level, this book was printed in South Carolina on American-made paper and manufactured entirely in the United States.

This book carries the accredited Forest Stewardship Council (FSC) label and is printed on 100 percent FSC-certified paper. Products carrying the FSC label are independently certified to assure consumers that they come from forests that are managed to meet the social, economic, and ecological needs of present and future generations.

FSC
Mixed Sources
Product group from well-managed
forests and other controlled sources

Cert no. SW-COC-001530
www.fsc.org
© 1996 Forest Stewardship Council

Find Your Place in History.